A HANDBOOK FOR NOOBIES

What is the Blockchain?
How to X (fka Twitter)
How to go to Crypto/NFT Events

SANDRA ABRAMS

TABLE OF CONTENTS

INTRODUCTION

Hi my name is Sandra and I'm a senior citizen who's passionate about embracing the future and making an impact on society. As the largest and fastest growing population group seniors have a unique opportunity to shape the future but we need to adapt to the changes happening around us. That's why I decided to dive headfirst into the world of NFT's and cryptocurrency, and boy am I glad I did. It all started with a TikTok video that piqued my curiosity. I had invested in Bitcoin back in 2016 but got scared off by negative media stories and withdrew my investment. Fast forward to August 2021 and I found myself drawn to the art world of NFTS. As someone with a background in nonprofit work I wanted to use my newfound knowledge to help my coworkers in the restaurant industry by creating and selling NFT's of my old photos but I quickly realized I had a lot to learn about this new world of non fungible tokens, so I got serious about my education and created my own curriculum in February 2022. After months of dedicated research and learning, I'm excited to share what I've discovered with other seniors and their families. I've put together this educational booklet that covers the basics of web three and I also have been sharing my knowledge through YouTube shorts, TikTok videos, on Twitter & Geneva. I believe that seniors can be a powerful force for change in our society, and it's up to us to get empowered and proactive. This booklet is just the beginning and I'm committed to continuing my own learning and sharing even more with others. I hope you join me on this exciting journey into the world of web 3.

CHAPTER 1

WHAT IS WEB 1, 2, 3?

Web 1, 2, and 3 are three distinct phases in the evolution of the Internet. Web 1 refers to the initial stage, or users navigated to individual static web pages via open protocols. In web 2, the Internet became centralized with commerce and communication taking place on closed corporate owned platforms. Web 3, on the other hand, is a decentralized online environment based on blockchain technology. As the general public gained access to the Internet web two emerged, serving primarily for information exchange. However, it eventually evolved into a multi corporate owned platform with a focus on e commerce. Users were bombarded with outside advertisements and content flowing through their daily feeds on social media and unsolicited emails. The rapid growth of e-commerce over the last few years, especially during the pandemic, led to concerns about personal data, privacy, and security with blockchain technology becoming more mainstream, web three emerged as a solution to these concerns. Decentralization, ownership, and control over personal data and finances are the main features of web 3.

Virtual reality is a simulated 3D environment that enables users to explore and interact with a virtual space using a helmet and gloves with sensors it approximates an alternate reality allowing users to experience an immersive and interactive environment. Imagine walking into the grocery store sitting in your living room.

Immersive virtual reality is the presentation of an artificial environment that convincingly replaces the user's real-world surroundings.

It enables users to fully engage with the created environment, manipulating and interacting with it using visual and sound technologies from other centuries.

The term Metaverse is a buzzword that has emerged in the web 3 era referring to a 3 dimensional virtual space where people can play work or shop like in real life metaverse is often used to encompass everything happening within the web 3 ecosystem including NFTS, cryptocurrency, virtual land, and fashion. While web 3 is associated with NFTS, cryptocurrency and digital money, Metaverse is more commonly associated with gaming and fashion.

As technology and software continue to evolve it is crucial to stay up to date with new developments. Familiarity with new technologies will become increasingly important as the world become more interconnected and reliant on digital platforms. The more advanced the technology, the more critical it is to learn about it, to stay relevant in businesses and society.

CHAPTER 2
WHAT IS AN NFT?

What is an NFT? An NFT is a global digital rules based immutable property rights system. Let's break that down. We see how the digital world has created globalization of business and how business practices are done over the Internet and the digital space. What is rules based immutable? Rules based is another way of saying computer code or a set of rules. Immutable is defined as it is not capable or susceptible to change. Property rights system is proof of ownership of a digital certificate. An NFT is a digital record or asset on a global platform with unique code that has a proof of authenticity which cannot be denied. You thought I was going to say Bored Ape Yacht Club and yes, NFTs can be art and media collectibles, medical records, mortgages, loyalty programs, club memberships, season tickets for sporting events, anything you consider can become an NFT. We are moving towards digital communication and everything we do so it's imperative to understand NFT's are just that; digital communication. This digital communication is put on the blockchain and NFT's live on the blockchain.

It is put on the blockchain through a smart contract and the creator who makes the smart contract is the one creating what the result will be. And NFT can come in a variety of forms categories and properties. The most familiar category of NFTS is arts and media. The photography creative artwork and large series with large projects and one of one artist. The media is moving with music utilizing NFTS. As we move forward, we will explore this category further. When you ask what is an

NFT and I say it can be a variety of things and a variety of categories you ask what do you mean. I look at how the NFT is created; behind the artwork is a computer software program. Do you look at how the results are beautiful, unique, and different and wonder how that is created? A smart contract enables the creator to design command and instruct the end result of what an NFT becomes.

As a senior citizen I have been looking into this category of senior citizen documents and blockchain technology. It is possible there are companies that have access and the technology to do senior citizen documentation on the blockchain as a smart contract that you can dictate, you write, you make the instructions with the end results of an immutable authentic document, an NFT. An example of a senior citizen document on the blockchain would be medical life insurance, medical history. As a senior citizen knowing the cost and the benefits clearly, transparently and that they are immutable is a comfort just in of itself.

Another example for a senior citizen is putting a trust fund, college fund on the blockchain for grandchildren. No one can contest the financial benefit or change that or who the beneficiary would be. I see that as a benefit of the blockchain itself. As more people see the benefits of NFT's, the categories expand. Entertainment, real estate, and finances are just a few. I foresee in the near future more businesses will move towards utilizing the document of an NFT as proof of authenticity of the sale of their products and create loyalty programs and token driven communities in return. As I learn, I will expand my studies and stay up to date on NFT's, non-fungible tokens. As the world becomes increasingly digital, it is essential to stay up to date with the latest technologies and innovations.

CHAPTER 3

WHAT IS BLOCKCHAIN, ACCORDING TO SATOSHI

What is blockchain? blockchain is a digital Ledger of transactions that is decentralized, distributed, and immutable. It is a technology that allows for secure, transparent, and tamper proof record keeping. According to the book of Satoshi, you can think of blockchain as a giant accounting book with a series of transactions. The Bitcoin blockchain is a public Ledger that uses distributed Ledger technology there are different types of distributed Ledger technology. Permissioned ledgers require users to have permission to access certain features and functions, while permissionless ledgers allow anyone to join, and access all features and functions. Hybrid ledgers combine elements of both.

As a digital currency Bitcoin uses the blockchain to enable constant transactions. The public Ledger grows daily as new transactions are added. Each block in the blockchain contains information that is unique and fits together like pieces in a puzzle. Next line to ensure the accuracy of each transaction, a timestamp is added to each block. This timestamp serves as proof of the authenticity of the information and allows the puzzle pieces to fit together correctly.

Bitcoin is unique in that it not only uses the blockchain as a software program, but it is also a digital currency that exists on top of the blockchain. As blockchain technology continues to evolve and become more widely adopted, it has the potential to transform industries and the way we conduct our finances.

CHAPTER 4
WHAT IS TOKENOMICS?

Tokenomics refers to the economic factors that influence a token's use and value. Similar to how central banks have monetary policies, blockchain projects create rules around their tokens. However, unlike traditional monetary policies, Tokenomics rules are carried out through code and are predictable, transparent, and difficult to change.

The supply and demand of tokens are the primary factors that impact their price. Tokens have a maximum and circulating supply, which give an idea of how many tokens will ultimately exist.

Tokens can be used for various purposes, including governance, stable coins for currency, and security tokens as financial assets. Tokenization of traditional assets will generate new tokenomics models in the future, and token economies and protocols are expected to become the norm in mainstream society.

Cryptocurrencies, like Bitcoin and Ethereum, are being used for financial transactions, blockchain storage and computing powers, governance, and securities. The applications of cryptocurrencies and their tokens are constantly changing with advancement in technology.

As commerce moves towards utilizing tokens within the business world, token communities that accept other ecosystem tokens and vice versa will grow the assets value and demand. Understanding the basics of tokenomics and all the different types of cryptocurrencies is useful, as this monetary system is becoming increasingly relevant in everyday business.

CHAPTER 5

MARKETPLACES & CRYPTO WALLETS

Marketplaces for NFTS are similar to other online marketplaces such as Amazon, which offers a variety of products and memberships with different benefits. NFT marketplaces also offer a variety of products, including arts and media, sports memorabilia, and other categories of NFT's. Some marketplaces are for members to display their NFTS, and the costs vary. The cost is considered gas fees, which is analogous to administration fees, delivery fees, and taxes on Amazon. However the outcome of the two types of marketplaces are vastly different.

There are several marketplaces to purchase NFT's, such as OpenSea, Foundation, and SolSea; these are a few. These marketplaces have a variety of artists and genres and give you an opportunity to learn the story of the seller and what is behind the NFT itself. When you purchase an NFT, you're not just purchasing the art and media but also a unique experience that cannot be replicated.

In the world of cryptocurrency, wallets are online and offline vehicles used to store, trade, by, or sell cryptocurrency and NFT's. Keys, which are another word for passwords, are used to enter the wallets. Some wallets only carry certain cryptocurrencies so it may be necessary to have multiple wallets. Coinbase is considered an entry level wallet because it is user friendly and has simple steps to purchase or sell cryptocurrency. It has a variety of cryptocurrencies to buy or trade along with a section for NFTs.

MetaMask is also a common user friendly wallet that accepts a variety of cryptocurrencies, including NFT's. There are online and offline wallets, and hard wallets, such as Ledger, a physical drive that contains your account. An offline wallet like Ledger is considered a safe way to store and hold your cryptocurrency. It is important to be cautious when using cryptocurrency, as with any financial system, as some scamming sites can entice users with links that can steal their money, cryptocurrency. While MetaMask and Coinbase are generally considered safe, it's always good practice to take precautions when dealing with financial transactions.

CHAPTER 6
WEB3 & SENIOR CITIZENS

By using blockchain technology and smart contracts, senior citizens can create rules that cannot be changed, ensuring that their intentions are carried out. Non fungible tokens, or NFTS, are created through smart contracts, representing an immutable property rights system that provides transparency and clarity for all involved. NFT's can be used for medical documents financial assets as in trust or even art and media.

It's crucial for seniors to learn how to put their documentation on the blockchain as we move forward in society. There are zero knowledge proof companies available for access only records, and medical data companies can put medical records on chain. As the medical field becomes more digital diagnostic oriented, direct digital communication will increase, giving seniors access to data more efficiently and inexpensively.

Many businesses are adopting blockchain technology and its associated software in all areas. The principles of inclusiveness and impact are valued globally, and cryptocurrency is becoming an accepted way of doing business. This will help bring financial stability and overall well being to people, regardless of their background, financial situation, or location.

Non fungible tokens can be used to document a seniors finances, providing a secure feeling when leaving finances to loved ones. Smart contracts can include any and all specific information you wish to convey, such as the distribution of trust funds after your passing. These contracts are transparent and immutable, ensuring that your wishes are carried out.

In the future, mortgages, land titles, property mortgages, bank loans, and even senior citizen housing could become on chain as normal practices. This would provide authenticity, fixed costs, HOA fees, amenities, and secured transparent ownership. Token communities utilizing blockchain technology may allow senior citizens to feel empowered and safe, knowing they have a home to reside in.

For senior dependent living, smart contracts can protect seniors by providing clear directives for their medical needs. If at some point a senior cannot communicate their wishes or medical needs, having an immutable contract created while healthy can be used as a measure. There are numerous actions and documentations that can be taken to protect and empower senior citizens in their housing needs and medical care.

Businesses, financial institutions, governments, and everyday people will be adopting these technologies in the near future. It is imperative to learn and keep up with what's happening; your future depends on it.

CHAPTER 7

HOW TO X

(fka Twitter)

By Sandra Abrams Onboard60

(Founder)

My name is Sandra, I'm a senior citizen, and I've been on X (fka Twitter) since 2009. A lot has changed. It started as a place for indie music, photography, Caturday pictures and Vine re-posts. The format was simple. You tweet, you like other tweets, you follow, you laugh, cry, have convos and become friends. I would see the same people daily and we built lasting relationships. We knew about each other's lives. X (fka Twitter) now has a plethora of timelines; political, financial, regional, technology, cryptocurrency, NFTs, and more. X Spaces have become a way to connect in real time. X Spaces can be informative, educational, focused on mental health, finances, news and so many more categories and types of Twitter Spaces.

I admit when I first came upon the NFT timeline and X Spaces, it was intimidating. Even though I had been on X (fka Twitter) for years, X Spaces added a new layer of connection. Initially ,for about 2 months, I would join different X Spaces and listen, not raise my hand, not speak, not follow others in the space, just be voyeuristic. I had a pen and paper every X Space to write down new terminology, a particular subject being discussed, links and websites, people that were suggested to follow. I started clicking on people who were also in the X Spaces, looking at their profiles, learning about them, and following quite a few. In one X

Space, after about 2 months, I was asked to share what I needed support with and what I was working on, I almost fell out!!!I spoke as fast as I could because I thought I was being timed (don't know why)and to this day, I could not tell you what I said. I did feel elated, accomplished. I spoke in a X, Twitter Space!!!! The invisible barrier seemed to be lifted and I was on my way. I joined X Spaces regularly, spoke regularly, and started to host some X Spaces.

This portion is about X Spaces. The idea is to get involved or just show up on X Spaces, eventually, connections are made and in time you are just as active and a part of the NFT, WEB3 X timeline and have lasting relationships as you grow on your journey.

Be fabulous,
Sandra

HOW TO X (FKA TWITTER) SPACE

The rule of thumb is the X Space host is more of a guide and moderator, however, it seems that not many people speak if needed and hosts carry spaces more so than not.

**Types of Spaces (I'm sure there are many more,
but this is just a few)**

A good host share authentically and transparently. A good host lets others speak, lets them shine. A good host encourages and supports those in the space. A good host steers the conversation to bring out the most value for all in the space.

Topic, discussion, current events & news reports: All spaces have standardized formats. Some Spaces are hosted by communities, some a few people who collaborated to hold the Space. Overall, anyone can open a Space for any reason.

Topic: Host either has the information, knowledge & experience or people in the space have the information, knowledge & experience on the topic being discussed. There is always active searching on search engines during Spaces that people avail themselves to, along with the alpha being dropped. Topic Spaces are either educational in nature or just fun facts, maybe nature or a common interest of those in the Space.

Discussion: These Spaces seem to be more fluid in nature, discussions may cover a plethora of subjects or may be for groups/issues. Spaces can be used for mental health, arts & media NFTs, morning/daily shows and professional/personal support.

News & Current events: These spaces can be 15 minutes for daily news blurbs to hours to days on end discussing a particular news event such as FTX and SBF.

ALWAYS HAVE PEN AND PAPER TO WRITE DOWN ALPHA OR ANY INFO YOU HEAR

Hosting:

Moderator: Have prepared articles, paragraphs, information being discussed. It is imperative that you have enough material to carry the Space. I personally hold one hour time slots and stop on the hour. I have had to carry a room for an entire hour, and it wasn't easy. Big tip: have lots of water close by, take breaks when needed to catch your breath, drink water, and sort your thoughts. It's useful to remember that your big why to do the space was from a positive intention, enjoy yourself and relax.

Spotlight Interview Host: Have set questions in a story format that leads the guest in a progressive manner. The questions can be tailored to each guest and their story.

Standard questions:

1. Introduction of person (childhood, event that led them here)
2. Big Why they are here, their purpose
3. What's their vision? Mission?
4. Goals for the month, 3-6 months, 1 year?
5. What are some of their stuck points, struggles in the space
6. What gives them joy, what lights them up?
7. What are their accomplishments, what are they building- going to build?

HOW TO X (FKA TWITTER)

X (fka Twitter) is a social media platform where you can connect with likeminded people. Tweets scroll through your timeline, you can like them, reply, retweet, quote the tweet or just read and scroll by.

Vet followers/following: Initially, you do not know the follower or who you're following except in the tweets. It is useful to go to their profile, read their profile, scroll through their tweets and get to know if this is someone you have things in common, their tweets are something you want to see regularly, you want to build a connection, you want to follow them. There have been times I have followed misleading accounts, their true colors rise up after a few months, a few interactions, a few tweets and I have muted or blocked them. It is vital to feel safe on social media, vetting followers and who you follow is one way to stay safe. I ask myself, is this someone I would have coffee with IRL, have dinner with? If the answer is yes, I follow.

Tweets: It is useful to tweet regularly. Some tweet on the weekends only, some people tweet numerous times daily. I started tweeting a good morning daily and a good night nightly. After a while, I liked a few tweets, then commented a smiley face or another emoji. In time I was conversing with others and tweeting my thoughts and what I had for lunch that day, yeah, I know?!?

X can be a platform to meet like minded people, create bonds, share your moments. How to Twitter depends how involved you want to become and the time you want to spend on the platform. I suggest evaluating your intentions and plan to follow through. Once a day, weekly or dive into X Spaces. Be safe, be consistent and get what you want out of X by how you show up.

CHAPTER 8

HOW TO PREP, ATTEND & FOLLOW UP IRL EVENTS

My name is Sandra Abrams, I'm a senior citizen, living in South Florida, learning how to navigate through Web3. I share my experiences, my joys, stuck points, and accomplishments. I have attended a few IRL events with intention of learning and connecting with as many people who were like minded and on the same forward motion trajectory as me, with much success. This booklet is my step-by-step guide behind the scenes of how to get and give the most from IRL events.

I have attended 4 IRL WEB3 events. Each time, I learned what to do and what not to do. Initially, I was guided by my mentors. There was a lot to learn. This is from my perspective and from the different suggestions and directives given to me along the way.

IRL WEB3 events are exciting and can be overwhelming. It is useful to be prepared. It is also useful to have a game plan as to what you want to accomplish at IRL WEB3 events. Your intentions.

My first suggestion is to have someone more experienced that you can go to and ask if your intentions are realistic and get guidance. Are you going to hear speakers and connect with people at the event, are you speaking, do you have a booth?

My first event I attended with my mentors. I thought I was going to be a volunteer, get water, maybe get lunch, be the Gopher. I had no idea what I was walking into. I was asked to go on stage and introduce Onboard60. That was the beginning of so much to come.

IRL WEB3 events are unique. For the most part you already have a relationship through a social media platform but haven't met them in real life. I walked in anticipating with excitement to meet people in real life I looked up to and respected, for the first time. My inhibitions were down, and my trust level was high.

There definitely was a neon sign over my head saying newbie. I also know there was a lot of newbies there too. I was very fortunate to meet up with the people that I had built relationships with, and they made me feel comfortable from the start.

People were inviting and open, answering any question that I had and seemed genuinely interested in me and my project. Authentic & transparent.

LET'S TALK PREP

I would like to mention the emotional, mental, and physical occurrences that happened to me before & during my first IRL WEB3 event. I was a ball of nerves, anxious, fearful of the unknown & I had a big dose of the "less than, I'm not good enough", the if you really knew me fears. I didn't sleep much leading up to the event and stayed in my head magnifying my fears. I was afraid since I was a waitress with little to no money, my past losses in crypto & my lack of knowledge would keep me from being accepted. I was wrong. My fears were laid to rest with the first welcoming connections IRL. We are still connected to this day.

PREP: The first thing I do was check out the schedule of the IRL web3 event. This allows me to schedule the speakers and panels that I would like to hear. I look at the different topics that are being discussed and choose the ones that would give me the best value to help me and my project. I also check out the speakers' social medias to learn more about them. This gives me the opportunity to choose who I would like to connect with and spend time with at the event. I learn their projects and companies they are involved with to see if there have like-minded values and principles. I make a list and prioritize topics, speakers, and panels. I do this so I can realistically achieve the goals I set out to achieve.

One of my first goals is to optimize my time by scheduling the MUST topics, speakers, and panels. This includes the people I would like to connect with and build a relationship. Most of the time, I already have initial contact through social media as I follow them and comment on their posts and or they also follow me, and we have engaged in conversation through social media.

Now that I have a plan of speakers and panels, a tentative schedule to follow, I move onto some of my own DYOR. I read up on the topics and panels I did not choose and see if there are any I missed. I also familiarize myself with the topics before I attend so if I need to learn vocabulary or more about the subject, I do.

This way, I can have alternative choices or rearrange my initial schedule.

Once I am familiar with the subject matter of the IRL WEB3 event, I continue to follow and engage those I anticipate meeting at the event.

This is where I mention costs. These events can get costly, with the price of admission, travel, hotel, and meals. I personally bring food/snacks and bottled water with me. I experienced long intense days with little or no time to stop, eat or drink. Besides the costs of food, having my familiar foods was comforting. I was able to pay attention to what was happening rather than obsess over being hungry or thirsty. Prep for these things - attempt to get deals for travel and hotel along with bringing your comfort snacks. Did I mention water? Sounds frivolous but always have a water bottle. You will get thirsty.

Another important factor is your comfort. Flat shoes, tennis shoes are what I recommend. I walked constantly throughout the events and comfortable shoes were a must. I also brought comfortable clothes that I enjoyed wearing and felt good wearing. It helped with my anxiety. I felt comfortable so I relaxed more. I attempted to take out all outside factors that were causing me stress intrinsically.

This is the part I tell you I know iPhones are used for note taking, however, I brought notebook and pens. I did not know that the exhibit hall would be filled with booths of companies and projects giving out pens and journal books. I knew I would be listening to many topics, taking notes, and meeting many people. As a senior citizen, I write things down. It is useful to take notes anyway you are comfortable with because there will be a moment or moments of information overload. It was also useful to have so I could write my thoughts and what was happening around me, people I met, my stresses and fabulous times.

THE DAY OF EVENT

First things first. Relax, take a breath. If you are like me, you have a list of what you packed. This may be extreme; however, I am assured I have everything I need for the event. This is the moment things become real. The anxiety of "will I have everything I need?" or "Am I bringing the right things?" kicks in. The list allows me to be calm and lessens the stress of traveling.

This is a good time to mention QR codes are on all the social medias so when I meet people, I have them scan the QR code. There are now apps that can help you put all your medias on one QR code, I met someone with QR code business cards.

It is a simple way to connect, and I was taught to take a picture so later I could match the face with the medias. It helped me remember them too because you meet so many people in a short period of time, it can be overwhelming.

This is the moment you can relax Great job!

You are prepped and ready to go. What happens when you arrive?

My first action was to get my accommodations and put my bags down. It gave me a chance to gather myself before meeting others. I put self-care as my priority throughout my first IRL WEB3 event due to my stress/anxiousness with the unknown. I consistently did self-talk including affirmations, pep talks and assured myself I was doing well. My thoughts of being less than and not belonging dissipated as the event unfolded. The self-talk helped immensely.

ATTENDING THE EVENT

My initial connections were with my mentors. They were so accommodating and supported my deer in headlights demeanor with gentle words and kind accepting eyes. Once the fandom wore off and I was walking to the venue with them, I was still nervous, somewhat anxious but I felt comforted and knew I was in the right place with the right people. The jitters suspended for the moment, it was time to learn, to be there to help in any way I could, I did go as a volunteer to my mentors as I said earlier.

Once inside the venue, it is useful to familiarize yourself with where the stages, the exhibition hall, the bathrooms, the art gallery, and where the hangout and food areas are located. It was useful to know the locations of stages so I could plan accordingly. Some venues are very large and have multiple rooms for panels and speakers; convention centers can be confusing. It was nice to know where the art gallery was when I wanted to just relax and take a break from all the activities. It was soothing, enlightening and very enjoyable to see all the different artwork displayed.

PANELS, SPEAKERS: Get to the venue early. Prior to speakers or panels starting, it is useful to reach out your hand and connect. There will be people to meet and connecting is key. During the event I continually saw familiar (from social medias) people and some new faces. I started building relationships before coming to the venue over social media and connecting IRL was just the beginning. By the end of the events, I had contact numbers, emails, their socials, and selfies with them.

It is useful to choose a seat where you can see the stage, hear and they see you being engaged. It was important for me to do this so that 1. I stayed focused, attentive & listening 2. I felt a part of the moment, like I belonged. And 3.I wanted to be remembered (connecting is key)

During the talks, I took notes, kept my attention to whoever was speaking, nodding even. I wrote vocabulary I would look up later, questions I had about the topics and literally everything a speaker said.

Afterwards, I would go to the person who spoke and would engage by asking questions I wrote down from their talk. I would inevitably get their contact information, a selfie with them and a handshake or hug. I was engaging while gaining a new connection.

No worries If you're keeping notes, don't panic.

The overload of information and feelings of being on tilt is normal. Lots of input happening. It was useful for me to breathe, take my moments to walk away, collect myself and comeback, the art galleries were my answer.

ENGAGEMENT: social media plays a big part in how we engage. During events, I did many TikTok's & tweeted including others & the different events. This established my presence into WEB3 and connected me with others.

I also started a spotlight series at Permissionless 2022 and continued it at WEB3 Summit 2022. The idea -- I highlighted what the company/

person was doing by showcasing them in a short video I posted on TikTok. It allowed me to be engaged with others while learning and sharing the event.

While at events, I regularly went up to people and said hello. While at panels or listening to speakers, I would talk to the person next to me.

Engaging and connecting constantly, setting up for what happens once the event is over; the follow up.

FOLLOW UP (The morning after)

It is a "morning after" feeling, believe me. My first IRL & everyone after, the first day waking up after the events, I do feel like I am coming out of a fog of anesthesia. The events are surreal, waking up with an intense afterglow & a morning stupor.

The overload of information and emotional intensity of connecting with so many in such an authentic way in such a short span of time was more than I could process in a day.

Some events took a full week of recovery. I drank lots of juices, water and ate carbs, Bolognese is my favorite, by the way. I needed to fill up to prepare for the **follow up**.

**IMPORTANT STEP! NOT TO BE MISSED! GOING TO AN EVENT IS FABULOUS!
WHAT YOU DO AFTERWARDS MAKES THE DIFFERENCE!
Start here:
**** collect all notes, contact info, scraps of paper, iPhone excerpts, anything from the event.

I gathered all swag, pens, journal books, and t-shirts, yes, t-shirts.

Write down all the companies, cryptocurrencies, any brands, logos from all the swag, pens and other items mentioned above. You now have a list of potential investors, mentors, business & or personal contacts you can research on a later date. The majority have their email or contact info on their items; you can add to the list.

Get on your social medias immediately, thanking those you met. Wishing others safe travels, salutations basically, connect, connect, connect.

Share on your social medias what's happening, then take the time to regroup for the next step.

INITIAL FOLLOW-UP:

If through social media, send a tweet or DM over the social medias. I stated who I was, my project and "it was nice to connect, look forward to future connecting, thank you for your time". Building long term mutual relationships take time, take your time. It is time to build the right support group of people you want to connect with for now and into the immediate future. The mindset, values and principles of others are important.

EMAILS:

PERSONAL: Depending on how you interacted during the event IRL, formality and niceties may be the rule to follow. If a personal relationship is being built, it is useful to wish safe travels and let them know how you are returning home. Also, it is appropriate to ask for a future time to either do a google meet or zoom, facetime to connect.

POTENTIAL INVESTORS: Depending how much IRL contact you had at the event determines the media you use to re-connect. In WEB3, conventional avenues are not necessarily followed.

I have cold Dm-ed someone through Twitter who was the head of grant submissions. We had a Google meet.

Initially, with emails to potential investors, I use a professional style. I am asking for the requirements and category of their grant program. I keep it short, direct and to the point. I do a follow up email four to five days afterwards if no reply from them.

Investors want to hear from you. WEB3 is in the process of building and evolving. They want to be a part of the future.

******do not miss this******

A side note but most importantly, is to be aware of your intentions. How do you want to connect, what do you want the follow-up, relationship to be after the events? What you decide to do, where to go, focus your attention, is where the after, the follow up ,the relationship grows.

Events are a fabulous place to meet, join communities and collaborate on future ventures.

Satellite events, off site of the conference, are where connections blossom and ideas are created. There are communities, established and new NFT projects, companies with off-site meet ups and gatherings happening on an ongoing basis. Morning coffee & convos, Lunches, by the pool, end of day cocktails and so much more. If the conference has an app of events or they may use WHOVA, a chat and scheduling app for panels, meet ups & events, it is useful to access it to be in the know. Also, you may connect with someone who is your next collaboration.

SOCIAL MEDIAS: Be consistent with all new connections.

Utilize your medias to connect and build relationships.

I have built some rewarding and lifelong bonds with so many people. I also continue growing my circle - "the round table". I am fortunate enough to have some solid consistent connections. It is useful to regularly connect and support one another on this journey.

The last tidbit I will share is the practice of "yes" by GARY VEE

Don't get left behind, say yes, and get involved. There are ample opportunities for everyone. Saying yes was the start of me attending my first IRL WEB3 event and saying yes to other opportunities has catapulted me to where I am today.

Be fabulous,

Sandra Abrams
Onboard60 (Founder)

Onboard60 Community is like minded senior citizens who stay relevant and up to date with new technologies and beyond. We are virtual, mobile, and in real life resources keeping senior citizens connected one family at a time.

CHAPTER 9

CONCLUSION

In conclusion, as a senior citizen myself, I understand the importance of embracing new technology and the benefits it can bring to our lives. Web three and blockchain technology are two examples of these advancements that have the potential to revolutionize the way we live, work, and communicate.

Through my own experience, I have developed a curriculum specifically tailored to senior citizens to help them navigate this new age of digital communication, I believe that education and awareness are keys to empowering our community to make informed decisions and protect ourselves from scams and other financial pitfalls that often target senior citizens.

My project, Onboard60, is a community driven space designed to provide education resources, and support for senior citizens to learn and navigate web 3 and beyond. It is my hope that by creating a safe space for senior citizens to ask questions and share experiences, we can build meaningful relationships with our families and adapt to the world of today.

I firmly believe that this technology has the power to enhance our quality of life and protect us from the financial exploitation that many seniors experience. By utilizing blockchain technology, we can secure our financial and medical records, our last will and testament, and all other senior citizen related documentation.

Together, let's embrace these advancements and not get left behind. Let's work towards creating a better future for ourselves and the generations to come. Thank you for taking the time to learn more about web 3 for senior citizens and Onboard60.

Sandra Abrams, senior citizen

www.ingramcontent.com/pod-product-compliance
Lightning Source LLC
LaVergne TN
LVHW041222050326
832903LV00021B/740